Tricorn Books

Montgomery at /

The Battle of Alar   /er
sixty years ago - f   42,
was for Britain the turning point of the   )rld
war. As Churchill said, before Alamein we never had a
victory: after Alamein we never had a defeat. Though
on nothing like the scale of Stalingrad, it took place
before Stalingrad and was the first demonstration that
the German army was not invincible.

This is not a blow by blow account of the battle but
an account of how Bernard Montgomery came to the
command of the British 8th Army and how all the facets
of his particular genius were needed to bring about
this famous victory. After it was over the church bells,
which had been silent since the threat of invasion in
1940, rang out in celebration throughout the country.

The author

Roger James served during the Second World War as a junior officer in the Royal Artillery in the 50th (Northumbrian) Division. He was with them in the 8th Army's victorious advance from El Alamein nearly to Tunis, and then back again to Egypt to re-equip for the invasion of Sicily in July 1943. They supported, with artillery fire across the Messina straits, the 8th Army's landing on the toe of Italy on 3rd September 1943 - the first invasion of the European continent. Then home to prepare for D-Day. They took part in the invasion of Normandy, and after the break-through there, carried on in the British 2nd Army's advance through northern France and Belgium to Holland. The last action in which he took part at the end of April 1945 was the final liberation of Arnhem. In all these actions he was under the command of General Montgomery who remains for him a great hero.

After the war Roger James returned to Oxford to complete a degree in mathematics and later he became a medical student. Subsequently he was a GP in Portsmouth until 1989 - and from 1973 to 1983 a Portsmouth City Councillor.

Roger James

Montgomery at Alamein

TRICORN
BOOKS

Tricorn Books

Montgomery at Alamein
Text © Roger James
Design © 131 Design Ltd
www.131design.org

All images courtesy of the Imperial War Museum, London

ISBN 978-0-9562498-1-4

Published 2009 by Tricorn Books,
a trading name of 131 Design Ltd.
131 High Street, Old Portsmouth, PO1 2HW

www.tricornbooks.co.uk

Printed and bound in Great Britain by
CPI Anthony Rowe, Chippenham and Eastbourne

My appreciative thanks are due to Dan Bernard and Gail Baird
of Tricorn Books for the trouble they have taken in rescuing
and publishing this book which I wrote more than
forty years ago but did not publish at the time.
R.J.

Montgomery at Alamein

Montgomery took command of the 8th Army just ten and a half weeks before he launched the attack that became known as the Battle of Alamein (to some historians, second Alamein). It was the last of three distinct encounters fought over the same stretch of Egyptian desert in the summer and autumn of 1942. Together they were decisive for the war between Britain and Germany. Although the end did not come for a further two and a half years, what Churchill said later was broadly true (ignoring the battles against the Italians alone), that

before Alamein we had never had a victory; after Alamein we never had a defeat.

In June that year the 8th Army had been routed by the German-Italian Panzer Armee Afrika commanded by General Erwin Rommel at Gazala. Having been forced to surrender Tobruk, they had then fallen back some 400 miles eastwards to a roughly prepared defensive position running south from El Alamein on the coast where there was a station on the single-track railway to Tobruk. This position, about seventy miles west of Cairo and a little less from Alexandria, had been chosen because it offered the shortest possible line. At that point the impassable quicksands of the Qatarra depression came within about forty miles of the Mediterranean Sea.

On this line which could not be outflanked, the 8th Army withstood further attacks by the Panzer Army which was in fact at the ends of its tether, thinned out by the chase and far away from its bases of supply. Auchinleck, the Middle East Commander-in-Chief, had dismissed Ritchie from command of the Army during the battle and had himself assumed operational control. During July he set in motion a series of limited counter-attacks which achieved little but cost a lot in terms of Australian and New Zealand lives and British tanks. These attacks and counter-attacks went on throughout that month (the historians' First Alamein); but for the whole of August both sides, exhausted, fell back on the defensive. Early in August Churchill arrived in Egypt with General Sir Alan Brooke (later Lord Alanbrooke) the chief of the Imperial General Staff (CIGS), the professional head of the army. They had flown out from England to see for themselves what was wrong with what Churchill called "this brave but baffled army". Eighth Army consisted not only of British troops but incorporated a division each from India, Australia, New Zealand and South Africa as well as a Greek brigade. After a few days of inspection and discussion Churchill and Brooke ordered a complete change of the higher command.

Then in the small hours of 31st August, Rommel attacked the southern end of the British positions in strength. He penetrated the lightly held forward defences; but was then critically delayed by unexpected minefields, so that daylight revealed his main force in a very exposed position.

Montgomery, now in command, had with the great help of ULTRA* expected the attack and expected it

*ULTRA was the code name for the output from the cryptanalysts at Bletchley Park who were breaking the German machine code Enigma

to come just where it did. He was able to lure the attackers on to the main British defences, which were very precisely positioned on and around the Alam Halfa ridge. The defences held and the attackers found themselves in a kind of amphitheatre in which they were battered from three sides by artillery and dug-in tanks and very heavily from the air.

On September 3 Rommel began to withdraw and on the 6th he halted very nearly back at his starting point. His last chance of getting through to the Nile had gone.

When Rommel got a bloody nose

The battle of Alma Halfa - known by the troops simply as the 31st of August or "when Rommel got a bloody nose" – gave an enormous boost to 8th Army morale. Under its new commander it had fought for the first time for more than a year according to a pre-arranged plan as a single unit closely controlled from Army HQ. During the next six weeks Montgomery was urged by Churchill to go immediately on the offensive; but he resisted the pressure, insisting on the need for training and preparation, amassing and assimilating new troops and material, and measures, which could not be hurried, to ensure surprise.

When all was ready the offensive was launched on October 23 under the codename Operation LIGHTFOOT. The name was an example of Montgomery's heavy humour. There were mines in profusion underfoot.

It so happened that several thousand reinforcements,

of whom I was one, landed at Suez on the 22nd, too late of course to play any part in the battle. For by November 4, after twelve days of exceptionally heavy fighting, the battle was over and what remained of the Panzer Armee was in full retreat to the west.

Unique talents

The Army itself had no hesitation in giving Montgomery the credit for the triumph at Alamein. When they got to Tripoli three months later they were entertained by a concert party led by Leslie Henson, a top rank comedian of the day. But at the end of the show the soldiers turned their backs on the stage and chanted, "We want Monty!" And when a few months later he took a short leave, he found he was a hero at home too. As he entered a London theatre the whole audience rose to their feet. But historians writing since the war have taken a more Tolstoyan view and ascribed the success much more to the great build-up of men and material than to the skill of the commander. John Grigg, for example, has said that, with his preponderance of material, Montgomery was bound to win. In my opinion that is a totally wrong judgement. It was certainly not the view of the generals on the spot, and not the opinion on the enemy side before the battle started. Rommel, recuperating in Austria, boasted to an old colleague that with three shiploads of fuel his tanks would be in Cairo forty-eight hours and Stumme, the acting commander of the Panzer Army, wrote to Rommel "We're going to wipe the floor with the British". Calculations based on the First World War indicated that against stoutly defended lines an attacker needed a preponderance of three to one at least to be sure of success. Twice before in the desert, the British had had material superiority and yet they had let the victory slip through their fingers. This time they were up against enemy defences of a strength and depth never met before. In flat disagreement with Grigg, I believe that

nobody but Montgomery could have won.

He possessed a unique combination of talents, which were all called for in this unprecedented task. Unprecedented it was; and only once again in the whole war did anybody succeed in breaking through a comparatively short front, which was strongly held by the German army and could not be outflanked. That other occasion was the Battle of Normandy and there again it was Montgomery who achieved it.

First, and perhaps above all, he possessed a faculty described in these words by Goronwy Rees, a distinguished academic who was from time to time on his staff. "The difference between him and other commanders I had come to know", Rees wrote, "was that he actually thought, in the same sense that a scholar or scientist thinks". And an element of his thinking was the ability to reduce any military problem to its bare essentials, so that the solution was a matter of choosing between a very small number of alternatives.

The transformation of morale

Secondly, like Napoleon, he realised the outstanding importance in war of morale. Bonaparte had said that the moral is to the physical as three to one. Montgomery agreed with this and set about boosting morale in a totally original way. I experienced one aspect of this later in his career when, back in England in the spring of 1944, he was preparing the Anglo-American force for the assault on Normandy. He set out then to see and be seen by every soldier who was to go on the invasion.

He drove on to the field where we were drawn up in ranks at attention. There was the usual general salute with the presenting of arms: but after that all was different. The standard routine was for the troops being inspected to stand to attention as the general walked down the ranks, and you were to remain so, eyes front, staring straight ahead, even if the general should speak to you.

But Monty wanted ***us*** *to look at* ***him***. *So there was the most unusual command to stand easy, while he walked along our ranks, looking not at all at our boots and belts, only at our eyes. After his formal inspection we were ordered to break ranks and sit on the grass around his jeep while he stood on the bonnet and addressed us. His first words were - and I gather they always were – " My Name is Montgomery and I am your Commander-in-Chief". Second only to Churchill's, his was at that time the best-known face in England. But he introduced himself: "My name is Montgomery". This might seem to be an affectation,* *a phoney modesty. I think it was not. It was a most unusual realisation that the principal thing to be gained from a general's inspection was not from his inspecting **his** men but from **their** inspecting him, so that they should know who was in charge and get to feel confidence that all was well at the top. Monty always included something to the effect that: "Now that I have had a good look at you, I should like to say that I have complete confidence in you. I hope you feel the same about me."*

In Egypt too the essence of his morale-raising was getting himself known and letting himself be seen, together with self-publicity as a new broom firmly sweeping away the woolly orders of his predecessors which implied indecisiveness and the possibility of defeat. I had no direct experience of that fortnight between his assumption of command and Rommel's attack on Alam Halfa, which one of his staff (Belchem) has called

Monty's finest hour,

but I did witness the effect of it.

On our way out to Egypt we spent six weeks waiting for a convoy in South Africa where many British casualties from the desert were convalescing. Their mood was uniformly despondent if not defeatist. The Germans were just too good for us, they felt, in Egypt itself, on our arrival on the eve of the battle, the mood was totally different, we would be attacking any day now and we would win.

Major General Briggs, commander of the 1st Armoured Division, said later:

"only those who saw it for themselves could realize and wonder how one man had succeeded in changing the whole character of an army in three weeks."

Montgomery had begun this transformation of morale on 13 August, the day of his arrival at 8th Army Headquarters. His appointment was to take effect from the 15th but, characteristically, he assumed command immediately on arrival and signalled to Cairo to say that he had done so. He then sent Ramsden, the acting army commander, back to the corps of which he was also acting commander, (and very soon replaced). After that Monty went off to tour the Army so as to be out of the way "in case", as he himself later wrote, "there were any repercussions at GHQ", that is from Auchinleck the outgoing commander in chief, still in charge in Cairo until the 15th. This insubordinate assumption of command two days early has been severely criticised even by Monty's admirers, Ronald Lewin for instance. I do not think the critics can have realized what an impossible position Auchinleck had put him in. (It was Auchinleck who imposed delay, not Churchill who always wanted everything done at once). For Rommel was expected to attack quite soon. He might even attack during this interregnum with the army under the command of a locum while the designated new commander looked on. For Monty it was doubly impossible to wait because he regarded the current orders for meeting such an attack as a recipe for disaster. They envisaged neither a 'last man, last round' stand nor a strategic withdrawal; but took an uncertain course between the two. They included preparations for an eventual fall back from the strategically well-placed El Alamein position to the Nile. The whole attitude of the 8th Army, according to Kippenberger, commander of one of the New Zealand brigades, "was of having one foot in the stirrup." To Montgomery it was obvious that if Alamein could not be held there was no chance of holding anywhere further back.

In contrast with the widespread condemnation of Montgomery's eager action, there has been to my knowledge no criticism of Alexander for taking overall command of 1st and 8th Armies in January 1943 two days before **he** was authorised to do so. But everybody liked Alexander and he managed to escape almost any criticism until after he was dead.

You could have heard a pin drop

However, there **were** no repercussions; and when Monty returned to Army HQ that evening he addressed the fifty or sixty officers of the staff in the open air from the steps of a caravan. He was a small man, with a sharp beaky nose, a rather high voice and an inability to sound the letter r. He did not cut a very impressive figure, dressed as he was, in obviously new tropical uniform, with his shorts revealing very white knees - to the desert veterans, the cardinal sign of inexperience. Nevertheless, as he himself described it, when he had finished speaking: "you could have heard a pin drop, if such a thing was possible in the desert sand."

Years after the war was over, the memory of Monty's inaugural was regarded as a turning point in the fortunes of the Army. De Guingand, his chief of staff, wrote: "The address by Monty will remain one of my most vivid recollections. The effect of it was electric – it was terrific. And we all went to bed with hope in our hearts." And in the last years of his life de Guingand again referred to that talk as "brilliant, absolutely brilliant". 'Bill' (now Sir Edgar) Williams, another academic, an intelligence officer who became Monty's chief intelligence officer for the rest of the war, recalled the initial scepticism of himself and his friends. "We had this rather arrogant attitude", he remembered, "that we'd had rather a lot of generals through our hands. And this was a new one – but he **was** talking sense, although in a strange sort of way…this sort of stuff was straight out of school speech day. And yet…" By the end of this, his first acquaintance with Monty, his scepticism had evaporated. "I remember it was a feeling of great exhilaration."

Montgomery's voice, like Churchill's was instantly recognisable, quite unique and, in the years since he became famous, has proved more even than Churchill's to be beyond the power of actors to imitate. They always make it sound flabby, even effete. It was anything but that. It conveyed his immense self-confidence, his decisiveness, and his clarity - nobody ever misunderstood what he was saying. It was ideally suited to his short, sharp sentences, his cockiness, and his dry macabre humour. And what was really a defect, his difficulty with rs, became characteristically an asset. What might otherwise have been a typical haughty army officer's voice was softened by that impediment and conveyed both simplicity of character amounting almost to naivety, and the fact he cared.

No Belly-aching or wet-henning

In this famous address at Army headquarters he immediately resolved the uncertainty about the plans. There would be **no withdrawal under any circumstances**. "If we cannot stay here alive, then let us stay here dead". In the address itself and in other talks during the next few days he managed with unerring instinct (no doubt with de Guingand's help) to put his finger on what was wrong with the Army and also what was right. Wrong was the inattention to training, especially of officers, deriving from the assumption that experience (which was largely the experience of failure) was a substitute for the kind of training Montgomery believed in – rehearsal, for the likely moves and operations. Wrong were the vacillatory orders of which Roberts, at that time an armoured brigade commander, gave this example: "Before Monty we had Plan A in this event, Plan B in that event, and so on. Under Monty there was one plan, one task only, to stay where we were on Alam Halfa ridge."

Very wrong also was the tradition of 'belly-aching'. "By belly-aching". Monty told every gathering that he addressed, "I mean inventing poor reasons for not doing what one has been told. I will tolerate no belly aching". Another of his favourite terms was 'wet-henning' which meant continually making small adjustments to the position of the forward troops, making them move this way and that 'like wet-hens' in reaction to the moves of the enemy. There was emphatically to be no wet-henning. (He noted with great satisfaction during the Alamein battle that he had forced Rommel to wet-hen!)

Top hats will not be worn!

On the good side was the informality of dress, which a less perspicacious commander might have regarded as a sign of indiscipline. Montgomery recognised it as a manifestation of espirit de corps. It was a sign that the men, despite defeat, felt themselves to be in a privileged, elite force.

Not for them the regulation uniform that ordinary soldiers wear. It was something to build on rather than stamp out. Monty did build on it and soon outdid almost everybody in the eccentricity of his own dress. The photographic record shows the transition from the orthodox lieutenant - general's uniform on his arrival in Egypt (the only personal touch being the watch chain between the two breast pockets which he had for a long time affected), to the Australian slouch hat festooned with cap badges, and then the inspired choice of the double badged black beret which suited his thin foxy face so much better than the regulation peaked cap. Finally during the battle itself he was photographed without hat or insignia of rank and wearing only a sweater and slacks, receiving the captured commander of the German Afrika Korps. Already even for the enemy his face was enough.

But unorthodoxy could go too far. One day he saw a

lorry approaching him whose driver appeared to be wearing nothing at all but a silk top hat which he doffed ceremoniously to the army commander, who on his return to headquarters issued the solemn order: "Top hats will not be worn in the 8th Army."

A rendezvous for every fly

Army headquarters, when Montgomery took over, was located in a particularly hot and dreary part of the desert, a "rendezvous for every fly in Egypt", too far forward (in fact in range of enemy artillery) and nowhere near the HQ of the Desert Air force. In O'Connor's successful offensive against the Italians in 1940-41, the army and the RAF had worked closely together. But in the past two years they had drifted apart. That was to change at once. The air forces played a very large part in the victories of both Alam Halfa and Alamein, and cooperation was even closer later on when 'Mary' Coningham who disliked Montgomery was promoted and replaced, as Desert Air Force commander, by Harry Broadhurst.

Behind the inept siting of Army headquarters lay a slightly absurd hang-up from the first world war. All Britain's military leaders of the second war had served in the first, most of them with distinction. All had been deeply marked by their experience and there were two things that they all, Montgomery included, were determined not to tolerate now that they were in charge. One was the gulf that existed in 1914-18 between the squalor and danger of life in the trenches and the luxury and safety enjoyed by the staffs in their chateaux. Auchinleck had over-compensated for this by putting his headquarters in danger and making its working conditions so uncomfortable as to be inefficient. He himself slept on the ground so as to share his men's hardships. Montgomery, on his first day, ordered the removal of Army HQ backwards and northwards to the seashore where it could enjoy sea breezes, comparative absences of flies, and such proximity to Air Force HQ that officers of the two staffs could share a mess. There would be no great gulf if the commander and his staff were seen frequently among the forward troops and shared their dangers there. He minimised the gulf still more by making it a rule that promotion in the senior staff would come only after a spell in a fighting unit.

No useless slaughter

The second thing the survivors of World War 1 were determined not to repeat was the useless slaughter that had decimated their generation. For many of them the memory of it had the effect of shying them away from anything resembling a massed frontal attack. For Montgomery, probably because of that unusual quality that Rees had remarked in him, that ability to think things through, the operative word was useless. The object was to win, and a massed frontal attack might be the best and in the end the cheapest way to win. The essential thing was not to attack uselessly and never to go on attacking when nothing was being achieved by it. At El Alamein nothing but a frontal attack was possible. He could face up to that. He knew it had to be a 'killing match;' but he would make sure that it was not a useless one. In fact the casualties, though very heavy – a total of 13,500 on the British side – amounted to almost the same as had been incurred during the month of July, in what some historians are pleased to call First Alamein, the succession of small attacks that achieved nothing much.

It has been held against Monty that he positively enjoyed the idea of killing. His pep talks to officers impressing on them the need to get their men into a killing frame of mind are cited in evidence. Nobody who knew him personally regarded him as a sadist. Quite the contrary. But he did feel the need to counter the idea that war was a game, a mammoth kind of chess, that could be won by the cleverness of generals. He knew he had to impress on his troops that the battle and the war could be won only if they were determined to kill and prepared to be killed. It is a lesson that has had to be learned again.

But, curiously enough, Alamein although a killing match was perhaps more than most battles a game of wits, a game in which Montgomery consciously and successfully provoked Rommel into ill conceived and ill-prepared counter-attacks and made him "wet-hen", having studied his previous behaviour and guessed that he would do so.

'Change of Style'

In parenthesis, it is worth mentioning that Alamein was part of the larger Mediterranean strategy; and Brooke, its principal architect, in the same way put himself mentally into Hitler's Position. Brooke's strategy which played so large a part in the Allied success – and which the Americans never fully accepted – depended on his recognition that it was not in Hitler's character to sanction any strategic withdrawals. The Americans always suspected Brooke and Churchill (with some justice in his case) of pushing the Mediterranean campaigns in order to get out of the cross-channel attack. But Brooke's object was to weaken German forces in France by forcing dispersal on them and so making a cross-channel assault possible. The North African and Italian campaigns worked from the Allied point of view because Hitler could be relied on not to take the strategically correct course of withdrawal to the Alps and concentrating his forces on the Eastern and Western fronts. Instead he reinforced the Italian front from northern France on the very eve of the Normandy D-Day.

Scissors cut paper

Next in the list of Monty's assets comes his realism. His attitude towards the comfort of Army headquarters is an example. I shall mention three others. When Rommel began to withdraw from Alam Halfa, there was a chance of cutting off his retreat and surrounding his panzer divisions. Montgomery made an attempt to do this but, as Field-Marshall Lord Carver has written: "the disappointing results" (of the first counter-attacks) "showed him only too clearly how blunt was the instrument in his hands when it came to attack". Monty the realist, could see that to persist would gain him little and might lose him a lot of men and material. He called off the attempt. He knew that there was a world of difference between the standards of training required to hold a defensive position and that needed for a successful offensive, especially against such skilful soldiers as the Afrika Korps. Above all training was needed in cooperation between tanks and other arms. The recent desert failures had resulted in infantry and tanks having no faith in each other.

There was a dangerous schism in many British armoured regiments, many of which had been converted from cavalry. The junior officers were mostly wartime conscripts or volunteers, townsmen mainly, and trained from the start on tanks. Compared with their seniors who regarded them as socially inferior, they were technically expert. The colonels and majors were often territorials, horsey men from the country who resented the conversion to machines. Tanks were to them mechanical horses and their minds were geared to hunt. The Germans had, at an early stage, realized that the tank, unless it was static and dug in, was not the best weapon for destroying the enemy's tanks. Rommel had a kind of scissors cut paper philosophy in this respect. Tanks were to break through the enemy lines and destroy "soft-skinned" vehicles and the rear organisation; guns destroy tanks; and infantry destroy guns. However, he used his tanks as bait. At the drop of a hat, or rather at the sight of a retreating enemy tank, the British tanks were off, tally ho, in pursuit of the enemy tanks which skilfully led them on - on to a screen of concealed anti-tank guns which might include the deadly 88s, 88 millimetre anti aircraft guns adapted for anti tank purposes. Hundreds of tanks and brave men were lost like that. The British commands were extraordinarily slow to appreciate that this was a deliberate tactic. Wavell an earlier commander-in-chief had remarked on the "disinclination" of the German tanks to accept battle, apparently believing that they showed lack of faith in their own tanks or fighting skill.

They're after the fox!

Monty very soon saw how the British armour were still falling for the enemy trick. "They're after the fox", he would say of them, "They're after the fox", characteristically repeating himself in that way which, as Rees has remarked, he used to convey derision, malice, contempt, admiration or respect. It was left to the listener to guess which was intended. At Alam Halfa Monty turned the tables and substituted for the pursuit of the fox the slogan "Dog eat rabbit". The dug-in British tanks and guns were to concentrate their fire not on the enemy armour but on the accompanying petrol and ammunition lorries. The tanks could not go far without replenishment.

The romantic Churchill was rather disgusted when he heard about this order. It seemed to him somehow unmanly to shell the unarmoured supply lorries.

British tenacity

Monty was emphatically not a romantic; but his realism was not restricted to appreciating his own troops' limitations. Equally he appreciated their strengths. Auchinleck's orders, which he had inherited, called for extreme mobility, something in which Rommel and his panzers (armoured forces) were adept and the British on the whole not. Montgomery wanted his men to stay put and fight where they were and so exploit their own greatest quality, one, which even Rommel, admired - their tenacity.

Tenacity was also one of his own supreme qualities. With him it particularly took the form of not losing his nerve. At Alamein and even more in Normandy he kept his head when, not so much those around him but those back in England above him, lost theirs and blamed it all on him. Even if any general could have been found capable of devising plans at once so simple and so ingenious as his for Alamein and Normandy. It is almost certain that none would have stuck to them as he did in the face of his own initial disappointments and the cowardly withdrawal of political and (in Normandy) air support.

Monty's realism

Monty's realism was particularly illustrated at a crucial stage in the preparations for Alamein. About a fortnight before the battle was due to begin, Monty was told that the commanders of the 10th Corps and its two armoured divisions simply did not intend to carry out the plan allotted to them. They thought it too hazardous. With so little time there were not many options open to him; but he faced up to the fact they simply would not do it and modified the plan so that there was more of an emphasis on the role of the infantry, whom he trusted, and less on the tanks. He transformed an imaginative but perhaps over-ambitious 'Masterplan' into a much more basic proposition - a battle of attrition - and for this, as Nigel Hamilton his biographer says, "romantic historians would never forgive him". What he did was, implicitly to acknowledge his mistake in asking 10 corps to carry out too ambitious an operation, and to retrain 8th Army to embark on a prolonged killing match.

His realism came to the fore again on the third day of the Alamein battle when he experienced a bitter disappointment. De Guingand had been so bold as to wake him up at 2 a.m on 25 October because he sensed that the armoured commanders were again dragging their feet. Monty laid down the law to them in no uncertain terms; and when he was called in the morning for the second time with his cup of tea, the news was excellent. His firmness during the night, he thought, had paid off. All the objectives of the night's fighting, it appeared, had been gained; but gradually it transpired that nearly all the reports were unduly optimistic. In particular the 10th Armoured Divisions had for the second night running failed to get their tanks out in front of the Miteiriya Ridge where he wanted them.

His problem in this battle was the same as confronted the great von Moltke in the 1860s. Then as now defensive weapons had got the better of the offensive. Then it was the breech-loading rifle, which enabled the infantryman to reload without standing up. Now it was the combination of the anti-tank mine and the anti-tank gun. In the changed circumstances von Moltke had proposed that "the task of the skilful offensive will consist of forcing our foe to attack a position chosen by us... our strategy must be offensive, our tactics are defensive". That was what Monty was trying to do to get his tanks in such a position that the enemy would have to attack them "on ground of our choosing". His corps commanders wanted to set up another attack to try to get tanks out. Monty, the realist, resisted the temptation it would be even more difficult at the third attempt and would only alert the enemy to his strategy. No, close down this part of the front; begin vigorous action elsewhere at once. That was his reaction.

Command and leadership

It does look as though it was a matter of command and leadership; for 9th Armoured Brigade who throughout the battle were under the direct command of the redoubtable Bernard Freyberg, the very experienced and forceful commander of the 2nd New Zealand Infantry Division, did all that was expected of it - and more - in its two attacks at Alamein. In the second, a vital part of the final SUPERCHARGE operation, 75 out of the 94 tanks which crossed the start line were wrecked and 230 out of the 400 officers and men were killed, wounded or captured. Here Monty's iron determination and even ruthlessness were called into play. He told Freyberg that he was prepared to accept one hundred per cent casualties. The attack must get through at whatever cost, must blast a hole right through the German defences. It failed in that; but as one of the survivors said "We did make a bloody big dent." To the exasperation of the survivors of 9th Brigade, 2nd Armoured Brigade, who were under a different command, that of the 10th Armoured Corps, failed to arrive on time to exploit the success. This had to wait for a combined infantry and armour attack 36 hours later which did make the break that ended the battle. Monty's first action, when he realised that they were through and he had won, was to go over to the headquarters of 9th Australian Division and thank Morsehead, the divisional commander, for the marvellous work of his division, who throughout the second stage of the battle had drawn the full furious strength of the enemy on to themselves. (Their casualties were more than those of the whole Armoured Corps). Without them, Monty said, the battle could not have been won.

In the context of "useless slaughter", 9th Armoured Brigade's self-sacrificing attack has to be contrasted with the attack in July mentioned below in "First Alamein" when only 11 tanks out of 104 survived an attack which had no comparable purpose and in fact achieved nothing.

A month later, engaged in the task of gathering salvage materials from the battlefield while our division was held in reserve. I was one of a group who came across the scene of this incredibly brave attack and saw the wrecked tanks - at least twenty of them - which had been driven to within yards of the surviving German guns, having crushed some of them on the way.

How he was appointed

Montgomery did not learn until well after the war was over the full extraordinary story of how he was appointed to the command of 8th Army. After a round of discussions in Cairo and a visit to the Army in the desert, Churchill and Brooke had fairly quickly agreed that they should replace Auchinleck as Commander-in-Chief, Middle East Command, as well as find a new commander for the 8th Army. (Since the retreat Auchinleck had been doing both jobs.) There was little difficulty in choosing for C-in-C Alexander, although only ten days before, just before they left England, they had appointed him British task force commander for operation TORCH, the Anglo-American amphibious assault to be launched against north-west Africa in November. Alexander was then, and remained, Churchill's favourite general, and Brooke too had a high regard for him. For 8th Army Brooke favoured Montgomery. Monty had impressed him enormously during the long period of training the armies in England since Dunkirk, and also before then in the 'phoney war' and the retreat to Dunkirk, when Monty had commanded the 3rd Division in Brooke's 2nd Corps. Brooke had been able to rely on him completely. His diary of the retreat is full of remarks like: "Found Monty had as usual accomplished almost the impossible".

But Churchill felt that to put new men from England into both commands would be a blow to the morale of the desert army, as though implying that none of them was any good. Also he was as usual keen for 8th

Army to launch a new offensive soon, and he thought they would get on with it quicker if they did not have to wait for somebody to be sent out from England and then spend time learning the ropes.

Churchill favoured Gott, a popular corps commander who had taken part in most of the desert fighting. He was a dashing Prince Rupert type of general, more in the Rommel than the Monty image. He had in fact a record of almost complete failure. As recently as 22 July he had allowed to go ahead a tank attack which was every bit as suicidal as the charge of the Light Brigade. It had been planned as a combined infantry and tank operation and should have been called off when the infantry failed to arrive. Out of a brigade of 104 tanks, all manned by troops fresh from Britain for which this was their first attack, only eleven were capable of carrying out the order to withdraw when it was belatedly given. Yet, as Wolf Heckmann a German historian of the desert war has remarked, the brigade commander was sacked for carrying out his orders, while Gott the corps commander who ought to have cancelled them "was marked for higher things". Gott was in fact that kind of 'good chap' for whom every blunder simply adds to his reputation.

Brooke's knowledge of Monty's prickly and uncompromising character inhibited him from pressing his choice on Churchill. He admitted in his diary that he had been weak. So Alexander was appointed Commander-in-Chief, Middle East, with Gott under him as Army Commander. In the same signal to London, Montgomery, at that time commanding

South-Eastern command in England, was appointed to take Alexander's place on TORCH.

Tragic good luck

Gott then asked for, and was granted, a few days' leave in the Delta before taking up his post. He flew back from the desert by what was regarded as a safe route - the same as had been used by Churchill and Brooke a few days before. The plane was pounced on by German fighters and shot down. Gott died in the flames while trying to rescue the wounded soldiers who comprised most of the passengers. When the news reached Brooke he had no compunction now in pressing his choice on Churchill, and he prevailed. Montgomery, before he had even set out to take up the TORCH appointment received countermanding orders to proceed at once to Egypt. The Americans must have wondered whether the British were serious when Anderson was now appointed British commander for TORCH, the third in ten days.

With hindsight one is bound to see the tragic death of Gott as the most extraordinarily lucky accident that befell the British cause. It is more than possible that with Gott in charge Rommel would have broken through at Alam Halfa and reached the Nile. If that had happened and Hitler had reinforced him, he might have reached the Persian Gulf and threatened British oil supplies, and influenced the Russian campaign. Even at the time, Colonel Jacobs (later Sir Ian Jacobs of the BBC) who had the task of delivering Churchill's letter of dismissal to Auchinleck, wrote in his diary that Gott's death was a blessing in disguise. Lord

Carver, to me incomprehensibly, is of the opinion that Gott's survival would have made little difference to the outcome at Alam Halfa. But neither he nor any post war historian that I know of, not even one of Monty's many detractors, can bring himself to say that Gott could have pulled off the victory of Alamein. He simply did not have what it took.

Alexander, Churchill and Monty in the desert. 23rd August 1942

On the afternoon of 19th August, six days after Monty had taken over (and four days after he was supposed to have taken over), Churchill and Brooke motored out to the desert to see how he was getting on. Since making their decisions, they had been to Moscow on the tricky mission of explaining to Stalin why there would be no second front (invasion of western Europe) this year or next year either. Brooke wrote: "I knew Monty pretty well by then, but I must confess

I was dumbfounded by the rapidity with which he had grasped the essentials, the clarity of his plans, and above all the unbounded self-confidence with which he inspired all those with whom he came in contact. I went to bed that night", he added, "with a wonderful feeling of contentment...at last we might begin to meet with some success..." And Churchill, after a bathe in the Mediterranean from the new seaside headquarters, signalled back to the cabinet in London: "From what I could see myself of the troops and hear from their commanders, a complete change of atmosphere has taken place."

Affection which few commanders have ever received - or deserved

To continue with Monty's qualities: his ruthlessness in sacking officers from lieutenant-colonel right up to corps commander is well known, and no doubt some of these dismissals were unfair. What is less well known was his quite unusual confidence in his subordinates once they had made the grade, and his devotion to them.

The story told by General Kirkman is a fascinating example. In the summer of 1941, Monty had just taken over command of 12th Corps on the south coast of England. He turned up one day at the headquarters of one of his divisions where the officers were carrying out a sand-table exercise without troops. During the break Monty took the opportunity to give the assembled officers a short talk on the use of artillery. Kirkman, then a brigadier, was CRA, the chief artillery officer of the division. He had never previously encountered Monty who came over to him afterwards and asked him what he had thought of his talk. Kirkman said that it was all right; but he boldly added that Monty had left out the two most important points, say A and B. Monty grunted and walked away. Then, as he was taking his leave a little later, he said to the whole group of officers: "By the way, there were two points I should have added: A and B." A month or so later Kirkman was summoned to corps headquarters to take over as CCRA, the head of the corps artillery. Monty had sacked the previous holder of the post and promoted Kirkman. As he was leaving, the outgoing CCRA said to Kirkman: "There are three changes I should have liked to make here; but I put them up to Monty and he said they were nonsense". Kirkman asked him what they were and he told him, say X,Y and Z.

A week or so later Kirkman went to Monty and said: "There are three changes I should like to make. Sir". "Oh yes" said Monty "What are they?" "X,Y and Z" said Kirkman. "Yes, all right, go ahead" said Monty. The end of the story was this. When, more than a year later, Monty took over command of 8th Army, he asked for Kirkman to be sent out from England to be in charge of the Army's artillery. Immediately on arrival Kirkman was briefed by Monty on the plans for the Alamein offensive and he was told that it was up to him to work out the whole programme for the artillery's part in it. This was a month or so before the battle. Kirkman and Monty met almost daily; but Monty never once said "How is it going?" or "Is everything all right?" or "Do you need my help in any way?" He just knew that if Kirkman was not happy or needed any support, he would say so. As he didn't say so, there was no need to ask him. Kirkman summed it up by saying that in his experience no other commander would have so convincingly displayed his complete confidence in a subordinate.

This was a vital element in Montgomery's success, for his staff and his trusted subordinate commanders were, to a man, determined not to let him down. It was the same with the army as a whole who "because they trusted him and felt safe in his hands" as Rees wrote after his death in 1976, "gave him a measure of loyalty, devotion and, not least affection, which few commanders have ever received - or deserved."

Unfortunately Monty was not treated in the same way by his own superiors. After the first few months in the desert, when Alexander was nominally his superior but in fact did what Monty advised - once that period was over Monty was never able to count on the continuous backing from above that one would have thought his triumphant desert campaign should have entitled him to.

The First War background

The talents Monty brought to 8th Army were of course the fruits of his experience. In October 1914, at the beginning of World War I, he had come close to death. He survived only because the body of a dead comrade fell on top of him and shielded him from further bullets. His wounds were serious enough to prevent his return to regimental service. He spent the rest of the war, first in helping to train the new armies in England, and later on the staff. This experience and the enduring interest it gave him in training and staff organisation were invaluable to him - and to the army as a whole - in later life. His contemporary generals in the second world war on the whole lacked both the experience and the interest.

His final appointment in 1918 was of particular importance for the future. It was probably unique in the British army at the time. He was made chief of staff to the 47th Division. The British army did not have chiefs of staff. But Gorringe, the divisional commander, had seen the advantage of the German system and so, very soon, did Monty. He wrote to his mother at the time: "The general tells me in outline what he wants. I then work out the details and issue the orders...and often there is no time to refer back to the general and I take the responsibility on myself; for I know his ideas and thoughts pretty well by now". In the traditional British system a commander has directly under him the heads of the various branches of the staff: operations, intelligence, administration and Q (supply - quartermaster's). He, the commander, has to coordinate their activities. In the German system and the system Montgomery learnt from Gorringe the chief of staff coordinates the activities of the branches, issues orders on behalf of the commander and deputises for him in his absence.

After the second world war, a general wrote of Montgomery that "his successes in the field have obscured the fact that he had a positive genius for training troops in the mass". Long before Alamein made him well known to the public, his influence, especially in regard to training and staff organisation, had begun to be felt throughout the higher ranks of the army at home. Another general has said that the standard he set at 5 Corps (the command he was given in the autumn of 1940) became the standard for training the British army at home. As I have already said, Monty saw the essence of training as rehearsal; as soldiers of all ranks from private soldier to general practising beforehand what they would have to do in battle, the whole performance then being subjected to rigorous criticism. It may seem obvious now that this should be necessary; but it was not the accepted routine of the time. During the whole eight months of the "phoney war" when the British Expeditionary Force manned the Franco-Belgian frontier from the autumn of 1939 to May 1940, Lord Gort, the Commander-in-Chief, did not order a single rehearsal either for staff or troops in the field of what would need to be done when the shooting began. Monty, it hardly needs to be said, continually put his own 3rd Division through their paces and a lot of men owe their lives to the fact that he did.

Monty had only a short time to train 8th Army before Alamein. The crying need was for rehearsal of cooperation between armour and infantry, necessary for itself and the only hope of disarming the hostility that existed between them. The failure of cooperation was partly due to the failure to make proper use of artillery for the benefit of both - a subject I shall return to. The desert armoured commanders were appallingly unskilled in the use of artillery support.

Oliver Leese, who ultimately succeeded to the command of 8th Army, had been brought out from England at Monty's request to command the 30th (Infantry) Corps. As one of the generals versed in what Monty called "my methods", he was appalled to find that Lumsden, a desert veteran and commander of 10th (Armoured) Corps, was in the habit of travelling round unaccompanied by his CCRA (chief artillery officer), as though unaware of the help the artillery could give to his tanks. Training was vitally necessary to overcome the outstanding difficulty of the initial attack - how to get the men and tanks through the mile-deep minefields which protected the main German and Italian positions. The technique of lifting and disarming the mines at night had to be worked out and then rehearsed to the last detail. Under Monty's direction a special school of mine clearance was set up.

Clearing the mines

The right man in the right job

The general already quoted said also that Montgomery's use of the chief of staff system was immediately copied in other commands: "Everybody saw the merit of it and wondered why it had not been introduced before". One of Monty's first acts on taking over 8th Army was to change de Guingand's status from BGS (Brigadier General Staff) to Chief of Staff, and he announced this change to the assembled officers at that meeting when "you could have heard a pin drop". In effect he set Brigadier de Guingand not only over the staff but also over the corps commanders who were lieutenant-generals. Any orders issued by him were to be taken as having the Army Commander's authority. This system was an integral part of "my methods" and was of a piece with Monty's philosophy of putting the right man in the right job and then trusting him completely. The system freed the commander mentally from being bogged down in detail and it freed him physically to tour the battlefield and see things for himself, knowing that the chief of staff would act for him in his absence.

Time to think

It was this system that enabled Monty to go to bed at nine o'clock and sleep soundly through every battle. (When the chief of staff found time for sleep is not recorded!) Above all, it gave him time to think. "How can they ever think clearly?" Monty once asked, long after the war, of the political and military leaders in Whitehall. "They go to conference after conference. They rush from their desks to official lunches and dinners and then back again to their desks where the work piles up. They stay up till midnight. They never have time to think."

Pre-war controversy

In between the wars there had been much controversy in the British army as to what changes were required in organisation and tactics to accommodate recent inventions such as tanks, aircraft and radio. The failure to resolve the controversy greatly delayed the production of some of the weapons that proved to be necessary, notably effective tanks, anti-tank guns and, to a lesser extent, self-propelled field guns. Broadly speaking the army was split between conservatives who believed no great change was necessary and the progressives who believed in the tactics of the breakthrough by tanks supported by aircraft and then a fanning out to cut the enemy's lines of communication. The 'expanding torrent' was the phrase used by Liddel Hart, 'the captain who taught generals', who was a principal advocate of the progressive case. The role of the infantry was then largely that of 'mopping up' the bypassed centres of resistance. This scheme of things required in particular that the traditional role of the artillery be taken over by the dive bomber.

Too often the theories of both factions were backed by experience in small-scale colonial skirmishes in various parts of the Empire. Latterly the progressives felt their case was more or less clinched by the spectacularly successful German blitzkriegs, first against the ill-equipped Poles in 1939 and then against the demoralized French in 1940. The Germans had in fact studied the writings of the British progressives, Fuller and Liddel Hart, and also of Colonel de Gaulle who had similar ideas for the French army, and they seemed to have put them into practice.

Montgomery never belonged to either of these schools of thought. In the twenties and thirties he carried on an intermittent argument in the military journals with Liddel Hart, who was a useful stimulator of discussion although his lack of practical experience made his ideas somewhat rarefied. Montgomery, though supporting the idea of organizing for mobility, believed in the traditional role of the artillery which had advantages that aircraft could not match. Unlike infantry and tanks artillery never needed to be 'committed' to a particular location in the sense of being irretrievably lost to any other. Without moving the guns themselves their fire can be switched from one area to another with great rapidity. Furthermore, unlike aircraft, guns are undeterred by darkness or bad weather and, once they have found their target, can be relied upon to go on hitting it.

Monty maintained that to try to turn the tables and use blitzkrieg methods against the well armed, very well trained and highly motivated Germans was a different matter. It would not work. Actually he did himself once mount a successful blitzkrieg against them - at El Hamma in Tunisia - but in a unique geographical situation.

Renown awaits the commander...

Churchill began a paper which he wrote for the chiefs of staff in 1941 with the prophetic words: "Renown awaits the commander who first, in this war, restores artillery to its prime importance upon the battlefield..." In the two years between Dunkirk and his appointment to 8th Army, Montgomery, with the powerful backing of Brooke, the Chief of the Imperial General Staff who was himself an artilleryman, and the technical advice of Kirkman, was the driving force behind the step by step improvement in the tactics and control of the British artillery, until by the time of the Normandy invasion it was undoubtedly the most effective in the world. It excelled particularly in the speed with which every gun in range could be brought to bear on a single target. On the way to perfecting the mechanism for this coordination, a demonstration of a new system of fire control was held at the School of Artillery on Salisbury Plain before a group of senior officers which included Brooke. All went well until an order to switch to a new target brought down a salvo which straddled the VIPs themselves. (Long after the war the author of the scheme recalled with horror the day "when we so nearly killed all those generals".) To Brooke's great credit, after he had got to his feet and dusted himself down, instead of angrily dismissing the scheme, he told its authors to go away and get it right. This proved to be unexpectedly easy and the amended procedure was so simple that it did not need an artillery officer to make corrections. The infantry, when necessary, could order "north 200", say, and so get the impact of shells moved 200 yards to the north.

The reason why the British system was superior in speed of reaction was interesting and surprising in view of the reputation for stuffiness, the Colonel Blimp image, which the British hierarchy could never live down however intelligently they acted. The reason was the decision to trust the man on the spot, often no more than a captain, to judge whether the target justified so great a volume of fire and give him the authority for the decision. In the American army the equivalent decision had to be referred back, with inevitable delay, to a general, a general furthermore who, unlike the junior officer at the observation post, could not see the target.

A life study

Montgomery once wrote that by the end of the 1914-18 war it had become clear to him that the profession of arms was a life study. By 1942 there was no general in the British army who could match him in respect of military knowledge and the amount of thought he had given to it. The first essential of leadership in his view was to train yourself for the job. You could not expect others to do theirs if you were not expert in your own.

As his competence grew he became increasingly contemptuous of many of his fellow generals and seniors in the other services who did not match his standards. "General Blank, a very gallant officer, a **very** gallant officer," pause "doesn't know how to fight a battle". This was commonly the form in which he expressed his contempt; or even more often it was: "Useless, absolutely useless. Ought to be sacked."

Even his most ardent admirers do not attempt to deny that he was quite exceptionally conceited and boastful, sometimes insufferably so. He was also unpardonably outspoken in his dismissal of the competence of many of his contemporaries. However Goronwy Rees does record this comment on Alexander: "The only man, yes, the **only** man, under whom any admiral, general, or air marshal would gladly serve in a subordinate position."

"Ought to be sacked"

But many of his observations about generals who ought to be sacked were inevitably relayed back to their subjects and so it was not surprising that a lot of people were gunning for him. But in fact his boastfulness and cocky self advertisement were akin to that of Mohammed Ali. For like Ali, he **was** the greatest; and their actions showed that those he disparaged **were** mostly useless and **did** have little idea how to fight a battle. Furthermore his conceit never conflicted with the interests of the war at large and certainly not with those of his own men. Indeed much of the boasting was to boost his own army's reputation. Notwithstanding recent allegations to the contrary (e.g. by Richard Lamb in his *Montgomery in Europe*), never for a moment did Monty allow his plans or actions to be influenced by the possible effect on his own reputation, still less did he care what history would say about him. The same unfortunately cannot be said of some of the other Allied commanders who have gone down to history as modest men. Eisenhower, for example, was constantly worried about his public image. Irked by the frequent use of words such as bold and imaginative in respect of Montgomery and Alexander, but never of him, he determined on quite foolhardy operations in order to change his own reputation with the press. Most outrageous was GIANT ll, an operation to take Rome with one airborne division, the U.S. 82nd (later of Normandy and Nijmegen fame), which had been allocated to support the Salerno landing by General Mark Clark's 5th Army. Eisenhower re-allocated the division to GIANT II without letting Clark know. (He also did not let Clark know when, after common sense had prevailed and the operation had been called off, the division became again available to him).   Eisenhower was also influenced by the need he felt for American troops to be seen to shine as compared with the British.   Montgomery, by contrast, deliberately and generously gave the Americans the most glamorous role in Normandy.

It became axiomatic with many post-war historians that all Montgomery's actions were to be interpreted in terms of self-aggrandisement; and many of them came to look for belittling explanations for his undeniable achievements.   His success at Alam Halfa and Alamein have been attributed to his merely implementing the already existing plans left by Auchinleck or to doing what he was told by Alexander. Both are as absurd as saying that Churchill simply mouthed speeches already written by Chamberlain. No plans of comparable quality were ever concocted for the battles under those generals when Monty was not involved.

Then it has been said that Monty relied totally on his staff, that the good ideas were their ideas.   All the members of his senior staff survived the war and all have testified that this was not so.   One of them, Richardson, has said that "it was quite clear to all of us that it was *his* brain and *his* decisions that were dominating the scene the whole time."   They have also affirmed that Alexander had no part at all in the plans or the conduct of the operations.   Indeed, as I have said, it was Monty who told his superior, Alexander, what to do.   Monty had been an instructor at staff college when Alexander was a student, and the teacher-pupil relationship was never completely reversed. Alexander had the good sense, except when later Eisenhower prevented him, to do as Monty suggested.

How battles were planned

Monty invariably wrote out in his own hand the scheme for a battle. Then he handed it to his staff. Their task was to work out the details. The idea of Monty carrying out a plan originated by his staff is particularly absurd in view of the rows that centred round him later. The operations that were decided on in principle at the big Anglo-American conferences or at Supreme Command level were invariably handed first to planning teams **before** and often long before an operational commander was appointed. When the commander was Monty, he insisted each time on recasting the plan and doing   it his way - Sicily and Normandy. In the case of Sicily he was only a subordinate commander and he had to make himself unpleasant in order to get his way, and even then he had to accept a superfluous tier of command with its headquarters. The size of the operation was right for one army. It was decided to have two so that the Americans could have one of their own, albeit containing only one corps; and so there had to be an Army Group headquarters above them.

When the commander was not Monty, the planning staffs got their head and the result was near disaster - Salerno and Anzio - or, in the case of TORCH, very disappointing - an elephant gave birth to a mouse.

His own comments on the planning for Sicily sum up Monty's character as well as anything ever written about him. "Alex (General Alexander) liked to do things by agreement and compromise", he wrote to Brooke. "This is very pleasant and everybody says what a nice person you are and how easy you are to work with. But you don't get what you ought to get. Personally I shall always fight for what I know to be right, and which means men's lives if you don't get it."

Battle half won before it began

Those who comment on a commander's performance are often tempted to concentrate on the actual battle to the exclusion of what went before it. In Monty's case the battle was always half won before it began, by his careful preparation, by his habit of putting himself in his opponent's shoes, by his gift for devising an imaginative but simple and flexible plan and for working out in advance how the battle would develop and how it would be fought and won, by the careful briefing of his commanders and his attention to the welfare and morale of his troops. Probably no one, not even he, could have succeeded at Alam Halfa on the plans left by Auchinleck, or on the plan made by Eisenhower's staff for Sicily, or in Normandy on the plan made by COSSACK (Lieutenant-General F. Morgan). In all three cases he, in Hamilton's words, transformed recipes for defeat into guarantees of victory. Unfortunately he was not given the opportunity to do the same for the invasion of Italy at Salerno, where there was at first near disaster and then virtual stalemate. When it came to the actual battle. Monty's most telling virtue was his quite unusual combination of firmness and flexibility. There must be a plan and he would tolerate no deviation from it; but a plan is a means to an end; and if it is no longer leading to that end modifications must be made to it. The commander himself must be the judge of that. He would not permit anybody lower down to say: "Oh, let's try something else", as for example when the armoured commanders at Alamein began to drag their feet. But on the next day, third day at Alamein, as I have described, although his corps commanders wanted to try again on the same plan, his plan, he said no. He would make a change. Discontinue attack in that direction, attack instead here. But the essence of the plan was not changed. It was so to act that Rommel would commit his armoured forces in piecemeal counterattacks which could be defeated in detail "on ground of our own choosing", and so to keep the initiative, to make Rommel always respond to Monty's moves, dance to his tune, and not the other way round. It was the essence of his philosophy of war - retain the initiative by keeping always "in balance".

Mischance into advantage

This was the sense in which he was right in his claim, so much ridiculed by historians after the war, that the battle had gone according to plan. But that bare claim concealed his own genius: his ability to modify his own plan, his refusal to get ruffled when his armour failed to perform the manoeuvre he had set his sights on. Never mind, we will try another tack, and that other tack could be tried without total disruption, still within the overall outline plan, still building on the success so far achieved and not nullifying the sacrifices already made. It brought out one of his maxims, one of the fundamentals of his military practice:

"You cannot always get what you want in war; the great thing is to turn every mischance into an advantage."

It is incidentally an excellent peace-time and personal maxim too!

Monty applied it even in his propaganda. His predecessor, Auchinleck, had been so worried by the image being built up in the minds of his troops of his opponent Rommel, as daring, the master of mobile warfare, and at the same time chivalrous, that he gave the rather absurd order that Rommel's name was not to be mentioned. It was true that before the advent of Monty, Rommel was the general both best known and most admired by the 8th Army. Hamilton records that Monty, within hours of his arrival in the desert, recognized that the way to overcome the bogey-man image of Rommel was to supplant it with his own. Bill Williams, Hamilton says, also noted the way the new Army Commander was prepared to use the personality cult of Rommel to his own advantage.

Rommel down to size

In the 1941 and 1942 campaigns Rommel displayed an uncanny "nose" for the desert. He always seemed to know what the British would do. In the Alam Halfa battle and again at Alamein his performance was cut down to size by his having to fight without the information he was used to. There had been a Colonel Bonner Fellers, United States military attaché in Cairo, who had taken a great interest in the British campaign in the desert from well before December 1941 when the United States had entered the war. Colonel Fellers enjoyed the confidence of the British generals and had been in the habit of radioing detailed signals home to Washington almost daily about British dispositions and intentions. But an Italian employee at the American embassy had burgled the colonel's safe and stolen the code he was using This accounted, at least in part, for Rommel's intuition. But a British

Rommel

attack early in July had captured an advanced enemy radio interception station, and this had given the game away. Colonel Fellers was packed off to the States in some disgrace. From Alam Halfa on, the roles were reversed.   Now it was Montgomery who "divined" what Rommel would do by reading his character from the portrait photograph that adorned the wall of his caravan. In Monty's case the "psychological insight" was supplemented by ULTRA, and this was a source that did not dry up.

Group Captain Winterbottom, who was in charge of the world-wide distribution and security of ULTRA was accustomed to being received in headquarters throughout the world as though he were the archangel Gabriel. He misinterpreted the fact that he was not so received by Monty. He took it, wrongly, to mean that Monty did not fully appreciate the value of ULTRA. It was just that Monty did not want to be bothered himself with ULTRA. To him it was one among many sources of intelligence, albeit the most reliable. But it was the job of his intelligence staff to digest all the information that came their way and let him know their conclusions. Also Monty probably knew that the very reliability of ULTRA had fatally misled Wavell, Auchinleck's predecessor, back in the spring of 1941, when Rommel first arrived in Africa. He had landed at Tripoli in February of that year with only one light division.   ULTRA accurately reported that the 15th Panzer Division would be arriving in May.   Wavell, not knowing Rommel, calculated that he could safely denude the desert force of his best troops and send them to Greece, provided he got them back again by May. But Rommel, being Rommel, did not wait for the arrival of his main force. He attacked with what he had got and swept all before him.

But at Alamein Rommel was outwitted by Montgomery without ever realizing he was being outwitted. He thought he was simply being out-gunned. This is obvious from everything he wrote about the battle, both at the time and afterwards. The very signal that was sent **to** him to recall him to Alamein from Germany betrayed signs of his own failure to realize after Alam Halfa that he was now up against a different sort of general and to impress this fact on his staff. "Enemy attacking since 23 October northern sector and since morning 24 October also southern sector", it said. "Intensification and extension of attack to entire front as from 25 October must be expected". In fact the attack had been launched simultaneously on northern and southern sectors on 23 October, but was to become, not extended, but increasingly concentrated on a small part of the northern sector.

Normandy repeated Alamein

"We're simply being crushed by the enemy weight," he wrote to his wife. Of course it was less humiliating to attribute defeat to the un-stoppable output of American war factories than to the tactics of a new British general directing his first offensive action. But his failure to understand precisely what had hit him stood him in bad stead when he met Monty again later, most notably in Normandy in June 1944. Indeed history repeated itself then in a fascinating way. Rommel in Normandy made some of the mistakes that he had made at El Alamein - worst of all, being fooled again by British counter-intelligence as to the timing of the attack, and so again not being there at the beginning. And Montgomery, in Normandy as at Alamein, became on the very eve of his triumph the subject of doubt and mistrust in high places and even demands for his dismissal. His maxim of making the enemy dance to his tune could be achieved in practice only by always remaining "in balance", another of his favourite phrases. It meant that you had always to have some force in reserve, and this in turn meant that whenever you committed your reserve to a new action you had to create a new reserve by withdrawing from the action some of the forces already committed. There was nothing new in this. It was a fundamental principle of war, and yet most generals paid only lip service to it. When Monty actually put it into practice four days after the Alamein battle had begun, he created consternation in London. The tension there at the time, and its sudden relief, are vividly described in Brooke's diary.

On the morning of 29 October, when it was learnt that the New Zealand Division and two British armoured divisions had been taken out of the line, it was at once assumed that Monty was preparing to acknowledge defeat. Brooke was berated by Churchill for not being able to produce one general who could win a single battle. (Brooke was particularly incensed when he discovered that it was Anthony Eden, of all people, who had put it into the Prime Minister's head that Montgomery was losing the battle. For Eden, in Brooke's opinion, had already lost one whole campaign by his insistence, when Churchill was prepared to be persuaded otherwise, on diverting resources to the militarily hopeless Greek campaign.)

However, late that night Brooke was invited round to No.10 for a drink and a friendly chat with Winston in his most benign mood. What had happened in the meantime was that an ULTRA decrypt had come in of a signal from Rommel to OKW (German supreme war headquarters). It said simply: " Situation extremely grave".

Montgomery, as Rommel clearly guessed, was in fact preparing to administer the coup de grace, Operation SUPERCHARGE. Similarly, after Normandy Monty was asked at what moment he knew he had won. "When I was able to withdraw three armoured divisions into reserve" he replied. It was at this similar moment in Normandy too that the murmuring against him grew to the extent of a campaign for his removal from command. On that occasion the leading mischief-maker was Air Chief Marshal Tedder who in the superfluous post of deputy to the Supreme Commander, had apparently nothing much else to do.

General Jackson, one of those post-war writers who appreciated Monty's genius, wrote: "Montgomery won Normandy as he had won Alamein by applying material superiority at the key points and never allowing any action to go on longer than was justified by the results... His policy", Jackson added, "seemed irritatingly methodical to his less experienced but more thrusting American allies and to his impatient RAF colleagues". To be fair Jackson should have excepted Bradley and probably all the Americans actually fighting in Normandy at the time. For, if the pace was slow before the break-out, it was governed not by the British but by Bradley and his First U.S. Army, then under Monty's command. But Monty did not mind accusations of over-cautiousness. For him war was a serious business, not a sport. The sole object was to win and with the least possible loss of men.

The turning point of the war!

On the morning of 23 October 1942, Montgomery's now famous order of the day was read out to all troops. Like the address to headquarters staff it was again couched in the style of the school speech day enlivened by cricket-field metaphor and an appeal to the Lord mighty in battle. It was intelligible to the dullest private and yet its ringing tone carried a thrill and an inspiration to the most sophisticated and hard-bitten.

Churchill, after the attack had been launched, wrote to both the Australian and New Zealand Prime Ministers, talking of the battle as likely to be an event of the first magnitude. But Montgomery, before it had even started, went much further than that. "The battle that is now about to begin", he told his men, "will be one of the decisive battles of history.   It will be the turning point of the war". His message began:

"When I assumed command of the 8th Army I said that the mandate was to destroy Rommel and his army, and that it would be done as soon as were ready. WE ARE READY NOW."

By pure chance, Colonel Liss, chief of the German army intelligence service, chose 23 October of all

EIGHTH ARMY

Personal Message from the ARMY COMMANDER

1—When I assumed command of the Eighth Army I said that the mandate was to destroy ROMMEL and his Army, and that it would be done as soon as we were ready.

2—We are ready NOW.

The battle which is now about to begin will be one of the decisive battles of history. It will be the turning point of the war. The eyes of the whole world will be on us, watching anxiously which way the battle will swing.

We can give them their answer at once, "It will swing our way."

3—We have first-class equipment; good tanks; good anti-tank guns; plenty of artillery and plenty of ammunition; and we are backed up by the finest air striking force in the world.

All that is necessary is that each one of us, every officer and man, should enter this battle with the determination to see it through — to fight and to kill — and finally, to win.

If we all do this there can be only one result — together we will hit the enemy for "six," right out of North Africa.

4—The sooner we win this battle, which will be the turning point of this war, the sooner we shall all get back home to our families.

5—Therefore, let every officer and man enter the battle with a stout heart, and with the determination to do his duty so long as he has breath in his body.

AND LET NO MAN SURRENDER SO LONG AS HE IS UNWOUNDED AND CAN FIGHT.

Let us all pray that "the Lord mighty in battle" will give us the victory.

B. L. MONTGOMERY,
Lieutenant-General, G.O.C.-in-C., Eighth Army.

MIDDLE EAST FORCES,
23-10-42.

days to make a visit to the desert front. But he reported back to Berlin in the evening that no enemy attack was expected before November; and General Stumme, deputizing for Rommel who was away on sick leave (thought by his superior Kesselring to be less physical than psychological), sent his daily report: "enemy situation unchanged".

So it was with total surprise on the German side that the attack erupted from complete quiet at 9.40 in the evening with an artillery bombardment on a scale not seen since 1918. By November 4, as I have said, after twelve days of exceptionally heavy fighting, the battle was over and what was left of the Panzer Armee was in full retreat to the west.

On the 23rd January 1943, three months to the day after the launch of the offensive at Alamein, the 8th Army entered Tripoli, 1,200 miles to the west. A fortnight later Churchill and Brooke took the salute there at a march past of the 51st Highland Division. "As I stood by Winston", Brooke wrote in his diary that night, "with the wild music of the pipes in my ears, I felt a lump rise in my throat and a tear run down my face. I looked round and saw tears on his face too...the depth of our feelings can only be gauged in relation to the utter darkness of those early days of calamities when no single ray of hope could pierce the depth of our gloom".

Only seven months before, Brooke was thinking, he and Churchill had been in Washington when, on 21 June 1942, the dreadful and unexpected news was brought to them of the fall of Tobruk which had previously withstood prolonged German assaults. The Americans had generously offered at once to send a complete armoured division to Egypt and Brooke had gratefully accepted. Four days later the Americans had second thoughts and offered instead 300 of the new Sherman tanks and a hundred self-propelled guns, without any troops. Brooke quickly saw that from the British point of view that was better and he again accepted readily. But the change was almost certainly due to lack of confidence on the Americans' part in the then British command in Egypt - probably on the advice of the egregious Colonel Fellers - and reluctance to put their own men under it.

Only seven months ago - and now here they were in Tripoli, further from El Alamein than London is from Rome.

That was the measure of what Montgomery had achieved.

Brooke, Churchill and Monty

Sources

Belchem, David. *All in the Day's March*, Coffins 1978

Bidwell, Shelford. *Gunners at War*, Arms & Armour Press 1970

Bidwell, Shelford. *Modern Warfare*. Allen Lane 1973.

Blaxland, Geoffrey. *The Plain Cook & the Great Showman.* William Kimber & Co

Bryant Arthur (Alanbrooke Diaries). *The Turn of the Tide,* Collins 1957, *Triumph in the West*, 1959

Carver, Michael. *El Alamein*. Batsford 1962.

Depuy, T.N. *A Genius for War: The German Army*. Macdonald and Jane's 1977.

Douglas, Keith. *Alamein to Zem Zem*. Oxford University Press 1966.

Grigg, John. 1943: *The Victory that Never Was*. Methuen 1980.

Hamilton, Nigel. *Monty, The Making-of a General*. Hamish Hamilton 1981 and *Monty. Master of the Battlefield*, 1983

Horrocks, Brian (with Belfield and Essame), *Corps Commander.* Sidgwick A Jackson, 1977

Howard, Michael. *The Mediterranean Strategy in the Second World War*. Weidenfeld & Nicolson 1968

Jackson, W.G.F. *The North African Campaign*. Batsford.

Jackson, W.G.F. *Overlord: Normandy 1944*, Davis-Poynter 1978

Kesselring, Field Marshall. *Memoirs*. William Kimber 1974

Lewin, Ronald. *Montgomery as Military Commander*, Batsford 1971

Lewin, Ronald. *Ultra Goes to War*. Hutchinson 1978

Liddell Hart, B.H. (Ed.). *The Rommel Papers*. Coffins 1953

Lucas Phillips, C.E. *Alamein*, Heinemann 1962

Macksey, Kenneth. *Armoured Crusader*. Hutchinson 1967

Montgomery of Alamein. *Memoirs*. Collins 1958

Montgomely, Brian. *A Field Marshall in the Family.* Constable 1973

Pitt, Barrie. *The Crucible of Wa*r. Cape 1982

Rees, Goronwy. *A Bundle of Sensations*. Chatto and Windus 1972.

Strawson, John. *The Battle for North Africa*, Batsford 1969.

Tedder, Lord. *With Prejudice*. Cassell 1966

Winterbottom, F.W. *The Ultra Secret*. Weidenfeld & Nicolson 1974.

Heckmann, Wolf. *Rommels War in Africa*, Granada 1981

Disclaimer

TRICORN
BOOKS